Andrew F. Hunter

Lake Simcoe and its Environs

Andrew F. Hunter

Lake Simcoe and its Environs

ISBN/EAN: 9783337182526

Printed in Europe, USA, Canada, Australia, Japan

Cover: Foto ©Andreas Hilbeck / pixelio.de

More available books at **www.hansebooks.com**

LAKE SIMCOE

AND

ITS ENVIRONS.

WITH NUMEROUS ILLUSTRATIONS.

COMPILED BY

A. F. HUNTER, M.A.

BARRIE:

Printed at the Office of THE BARRIE EXAMINER, 139 Dunlop Street.

1893.

INTRODUCTION.

EVER increasing popularity as a summer resort, growing importance from a commercial point of view through the projection of canals and railways, the ice industry and other features, are some of the reasons which determined us to publish the present handbook of Lake Simcoe. Our purpose is also to supply a want of authentic guide book literature, none of the existing guide books making any pretences to give details beyond merely general facts, and even these are often marred by mistakes. So far as we are aware it is the only publication devoted entirely to the lake, and hence its priority in the field will be an apology for its imperfections, of the existence of which we are thoroughly conscious. To several persons we are indebted for information and assistance, and amongst others to Mr. Barlow Cumberland, Toronto, who kindly gave the use of two of the engravings

Barrie, July 1st, 1893.

LAKE SIMCOE AND ITS ENVIRONS.

CHAPTER I.

GENERAL DESCRIPTION OF THE LAKE.

ITS PROMINENT FEATURES.

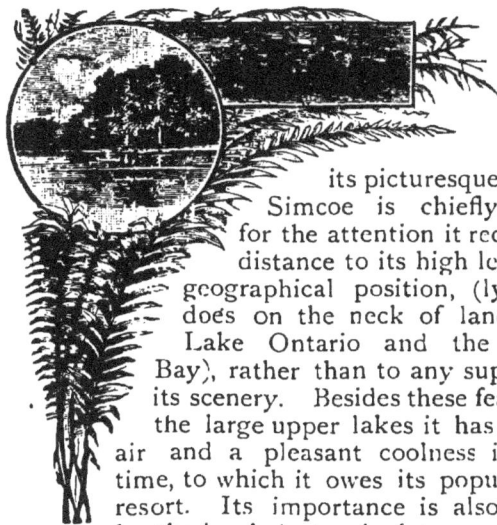

Though it is noted in some degree for its picturesqueness, Lake Simcoe is chiefly indebted for the attention it receives at a distance to its high level and its geographical position, (lying as it does on the neck of land between Lake Ontario and the Georgian Bay), rather than to any superiority of its scenery. Besides these features, like the large upper lakes it has a bracing air and a pleasant coolness in summer time, to which it owes its popularity as a resort. Its importance is also increased by the ice industry in late years, its projected use as a reservoir to supply the city of Toronto with water, and the perpetual agitation for canal systems in which it will naturally form a link. It has, too, an unusual number of historical associations, which add to its interest.

ITS GEOLOGY.

The rock formation underlying Lake Simcoe is Trenton limestone, which comes to the surface in a few places along the eastern side, especially at Beaverton and in the township of Rama. The high ridge at Beaverton is covered with drift to the depth of about six feet. In Rama the noted quarries of whitish building stone have been worked for several years. A very fine-grained and compact limestone, suitable for purposes of lithography, is found in the Birdseye and Black River formations in the same township. Besides limestone in Rama it is also found in Mara township; and shell marl is found in North Gwillimbury.

Few regions could be found more suitable than the one surrounding Lake Simcoe for the study of the drift or surface formation, which covers the primary rocks with a deep deposit of layers of clays and gravels. At Beaverton there is a species of clay from which an excellent grade of white bricks is manufactured.

The surface of the district may be conveniently learned from the grading of the Northern Railway. Rising as it leaves Toronto, the highest point (755 above Lake Ontario) is attained at the summit of the Oak Ridges 26 miles north of the city on the line of the railway. The grade then descends, but, passing through a gravel ridge a mile or two north of Lefroy, it rises again to 641 feet near Craigvale.

A breezy summit, situated on the ridges between the third and fourth concessions of King township, about three miles north of King station and four and three-quarter miles south-west of Aurora, is the height of land between the lakes. According to a recent account of it :—" On a clear day Lake Ontario is visible to the south, while near at hand the wooded hills and cultivated fields, dotted with farm buildings, and the sparkling water in the surrounding small lakes, make up a panoramic picture unequalled in the neighborhood. As a proof that the structure stands on the dividing height of land, Ferguson's lake can be seen about three-quarters of a mile to the south-east—its waters finding their way through a stream into Lake Ontario, while the sluggish waters of a pond of smaller area, about half a mile further north, flow north-west towards Lake Simcoe."

A singular feature of its shoreline is worthy of attention in this place. Many are familiar with the gravel terrace or ridge running around the lake at a short distance from the water. This gravel ridge, which was the shore of the lake in former times, appears to be about 48 feet higher than the present surface of the water. It can be traced around the entire lake, and it marks the height at which the water once stood for a great number of years, evidence of which is furnished by the large gravel beds at some parts of its extent. Around the western end of Kempenfeldt Bay, the terrace is not to be seen, which suggests the possibility that the bay used to extend through the gap of the hills and join with Georgian Bay when the latter stood at the same height. It is within the range of possible things, too, that connection also existed with Lake Ontario through the Holland and Humber valleys, as one of the ancient shorelines of Lake Ontario corresponds closely in height with this former one of Lake Simcoe, due allowance being made for the difference in their present level.

For other accounts of the geology of the district the reader is referred to:—

Spencer's *Elevations in Canada.* (Published by the U.S. Geological Survey.)

An article by Mr. Sandford Fleming in the CANADIAN JOURNAL, Vol. I., (First Series) accompanied by a map facing p. 223 of that volume, showing the configuration of the district through which the projected Huron-tario Canal would pass.

An article "On Wolfram from Chief Island, Lake Couchiching." By Prof. E. J. Chapman, in the Transactions of the Canadian Institute for 1856, page 308.

THE CLIMATE.

The temperature of Lake Simcoe and its surrounding district is much lower all the year round than that of Lake Ontario. To this is due, in summer, its attractiveness as a cool pleasure resort; and in winter, the superiority of its ice. The climate of the district may be seen from the following records for the past twenty years, made by Mr. J. J. Gillem at Barrie:

Year.	Snowy days.	Snow depth inches.	Rainy Days.	Rain depth inches.	Tem. lowest.	Tem. highest.	Hours sunshine.
1873	88	150	71	23.1	-19	117	2287
1874	79	177	48	13.0	-23	115	2161
1875	100	208	59	15 2	-29	113	2205
1876	72	139	69	16.3	-13	121	2269
1877	54	95	54	14.5	-31	118	2162
1878	80	122	105	27 5	- 5	114	2035
1879	94	185	94	18.0	-24	128	2142
1880	66	92	100	25.2	-10	115	2197
1881	56	95	87	20.0	-18	124	2354
1882	70	119	78	15.9	-35	116	2049
1883	74	114	103	20.1	-26	107	2013
1884	77	181	99	18.9	-32	116	2082
1885	91	134	85	26 8	-23	116	2163
1886	70	103	96	24 3	-28	116	1989
1887	75	137	93	16.8	-21	113	2092
1888	76	83	95	19 7	-22	118	2095
1889	47	91	101	24.7	-13	110	1966
1890	64	73	120	30.0	-13	117	1869
1891	52	79	104	23.0	- 9	122	2214
1892	67	99	114	26.7	-22	123	1991

As a rule, Lake Couchiching freezes over every year early in December, but Lake Simcoe itself not until the latter end of the month. Owing to its great depth, Kempenfeldt Bay and the main portion of the lake are usually frozen about the same time. The dates of the Bay's closing, as well as the dates of opening, for the last forty years, are given in the following table:

CLOSED.	OPENED.
1852—Dec. 31.	1853—April 27.
'53— " 28.	'54—No date rec'd.
'54— " 21	'55—April 26.
'55— " 25.	'56— " 27.
'56— " 16.	'57— May 5.
'57-- " 26	'58—April 17.
'58— " 17.	'59— " 26.
'59— " 13.	'60— " 12.

CLOSED.	OPENED.
1860—Dec. 13.	1861—April 24.
'61—No date rec'd.	'62—No date rec'd.
'62—Dec. 19.	'63—April 23.
'63— " 19.	'64— " 26.
'64— " 22.	'65— " 12.
'65— " 27.	'66— " 21.
'66— " 20.	'67— " 30.
'67— " 12.	'68— " 17.
'68—No date rec'd.	'69— " 29.
'69—Dec. 6.	'70— " 25.
'71—Jan. 5.	'71— " 10.
'71—Dec, 13.	'72—May 2.
'72— " 11.	'73— " 5.
'73— " 15.	'74— " 9.
'74— " 30.	'75— " 8.
'75— " 1.	'76— " 1,
'76— " 16.	'77—April 24.
'77— " 31.	'78—Mar. 30.
'78— " 27.	'79—April 29.
'79— " 24.	'80— " 15.
'80— " 9.	'81— " 27.
'81— " 19.	'82— " 13.
'82— " 16.	'83—May 5.
'83— " 29.	'84— " 6.
'84— " 19.	'85— " 6.
'85— " 26.	'86—April 23.
'86— " 23.	'87— " 30.
'87— " 24.	'88—May 1.
'89—Jan. 19	'89—April 19.
'90— " 14.	'90— " 17.
'90—Dec 24.	'91— " 22.
'92—Jan. 3.	'92— " 6.
'92—Dec. 26.	

ITS LEVEL.

At low water mark Lake Simcoe is 707 feet above mean sea level, although the exact figures are also variously stated at 714 feet and upwards. Kivas Tully gives 707 feet on his relief map, which he prepared as chief engineer of the projected Hurontario Canal.

Its level is subject, in common with those of other lakes, to fluctuations more or less rapid. The causes of these may be chiefly classed under two heads, winds of course causing temporary and local fluctuations.

(a) The condition of obstructions in the Severn River, especially mill dams.

(b) The quantity of previous rainfall. A great depth of snow in the winter of 1888-9 caused a rise of the water in the following spring. Lack of rain for some time will produce a considerable fall of level.

The fluctuations vary within a limit of about three feet, the variations not being so extensive as on the larger lakes. The water usually attains its highest level each year in June. As elsewhere, a succession of wet years will produce very high water, while a succession of dry years will produce very low water.

Within the past three years an agitation has sprung up partly for the removal of obstructions from the outlet of the Severn, and thereby regulating the level, and partly for the permanent lowering of the level. The advocates of the measure claim that 11,700 acres of land are flooded that should not be. A meeting was held in Orillia Sept. 23rd, 1891, to discuss the matter, which was attended by a number of Reeves and others from the municipalities surrounding the lake, and a committee was appointed. At the meetings of the County Councils of Simcoe and Ontario counties in the following January the money was not granted to carry out the object, owing to the expected interference with the depth of water in the harbors. The committee proposed to lower Lakes Couchiching and Simcoe to low water mark. A statutory low water mark, that of October 1st, 1889, as per Government survey is the standard by which this committee propose to regulate the level.

TORONTO'S WATER SUPPLY.

During the summer of 1890 and more or less since then, a scheme was widely discussed for the supply of the city of Toronto with water from Lake Simcoe by a large conduit. It was proposed to construct a tunnel which would furnish a daily supply of 125,000,000 gallons, and the advocates suggested the use of even more than this for power purposes.

The whole area of Lake Simcoe is about 300 square miles, from which it may be calculated that the daily supply above mentioned would reduce the level by one inch every 23½ days. In commenting on the question, the Toronto *Globe* remarked : " The advocates of a gravitation scheme will have to consider the question of the supply which Lake Simcoe can yield, and in connection with the question how the lake itself is supplied. It is fed altogether by creeks, streams and small rivers like the Holland, and the waters of these are not likely to grow either purer or more abundant as settlement advances."

Lake Simcoe has too much shoreline in proportion to the volume contained, to yield good water. Although it overlies limestone, which renders the water potable, still the large amount of shoreline for the comparatively small volume of water makes the quality inferior. Chemical analysis shows this, by indicating the presence of vegetable matter and other impurities, Respecting the amount of shoreline, the following comparison with Lake Ontario will be instructive :

Lake Simcoe has 300 sq. miles surface and 120 miles shoreline.
Lake Ontario has 6000 ,, ,, ,, ,, 600 ,, ,,

Thus while the surfaces of the two lakes bear to each other the relation of 1 to 20, the shorelines or circumferences have the relation of 1 to 5. Lake Simcoe accordingly, in proportion to its size, has four times as much beach per square mile as Lake Ontario has, thus rendering its water impure with vegetable matter and charged with sediment during storms. The greater the area exposed, in relation to the volume, as in the large lakes, the more thoroughly will impurities be oxygenized at the surface of the water.

PROJECTED CANALS.

Closely connected with the subject of level is that of ship canals to connect Lake Ontario with Lake Huron by way of Lake Simcoe, projects for the construction of which have been set afoot from time to time since the first settlement of this Province. It was across the Simcoe isthmus that the first Canadian railway was built ; and situated upon this isthmus, Lake Simcoe has likewise received an unusual amount of attention in connection with projected canals.

Mr. Rowland Burr, of Yonge street, near Toronto, was perhaps the earliest projector of the Hurontario canal, of whom Dr. Scadding in his *Toronto of Old* (p. 423) says : "Mr. Burr was an emigrant to these parts from Pennsylvania in 1803 ......A canal to connect Lake Ontario with the Georgian Bay of Lake Huron, *via* Lake Simcoe and the valley of the Humber, was pressed by him as an immediate necessity, years ago, and at his own expense he minutely examined the route and published thereon a report which has furnished to later theorizers on the same subject much valuable information."

Probably no course has been so much talked of as a canal route, with so little actual realization. Most of the projects have contemplated passing through Lake Simcoe.

From 1845 till 1851 Kivas Tully was engineer of the proposed Georgian Bay Canal. He constructed a relief map of plaster of paris, which is now in the Legislative Library at Toronto.

Thomas Monro, in 1857, was in charge of the

A PROJECTED SHIP RAILWAY IN OPERATION.

summit level survey of the proposed route ; and Thomas C. Keefer made a report on this project in 1863.

The Hurontario Canal project was a favorite subject with the late F. C. Capreol, Esq., of Toronto.   He was closely connected with the organization and construction of the Northern Railway, the first completed railroad in Upper Canada ; and for many years before his death in 1887, he devoted his energies to the agitation of the canal project,

Upon the recent discovery of the feasibility of Ship Railways, the canal agitation has been counteracted by an agitation for one, the cost of which would be much less than that of a canal. The leading figure of this project is Mr. E. L. Corthell, an eminent engineer of Chicago. The practicability of a ship railway to connect Lake Ontario with Georgian Bay he argued in an extensive paper read before the Canadian Society of Civil Engineers at Montreal, to which the reader is referred for fuller particulars of the subject.

" Many years ago," says the Government Bluebook, "the utilizing of the waters of the Trent River for the purpose of through water communication between Lake Huron and Lake Ontario was projected. The course in contemplation was as follows :—Through the River Trent, Rice Lake, the River Otonabee, and other waters to Balsam Lake, the summit water ; from Lake Balsam by a canal and the River Talbot to Lake Simcoe ; thence by the River Severn to Georgian Bay, the total distance being about 235 miles The execution of this scheme, commenced in 1837, was subsequently deferred. By certain works, however, sections of these waters were made practicable for local navigation." So numerous are the engineering difficulties of this route and so tortuous is the line, that it is very doubtful if the canal will ever be completed, notwithstanding that stretches of it have been constructed and are efficient for local steamer traffic and for the passage of timber.

An Order-in-Council was passed on the 8th of October, 1887, by the Dominion Government, authorizing the appointment of a Commission of Enquiry to examine and report on the question of the expediency of extending the Trent Valley navigation. Under date of Dec. 17th, 1890, the Commissioners made a report embodying the results of their investigations, and as further enquiry was deemed necessary, the Commission was continued in office.

CHAPTER II.

INDUSTRIES AND OTHER FEATURES.

THE RECEDING LUMBER TRADE.

IN common with the chain of smaller lakes east of it, Lake Simcoe is situated in what was the great Canadian pine belt. A brief consideration of this subject will be of value in arriving at a clear knowledge of the development of the district. The lumber era was ushered in by the construction of the Northern Railway in 1853, and for some years succeeding this date the industry absorbed a considerable part of the energy in the district, affording employment to a large number of people. By the year 1861, the production of this commodity had reached 200 millions of feet per annum, which was about one-third of the annual production in the whole province. At the south part of the lake, the activity in this trade was at first most pronounced and afterwards gradually extended northward. Among the earliest saw mills of large capacity was one established at Bradford about 1858. It was capable of manufacturing 150,000 feet per day or in the neighborhood of 20 millions per annum. Ranking next was the mill at Bell Ewart, which was, for a time, one of the most extensive establishments of the kind in the province. The kind of lumber manufactured in this region was chiefly white pine, which predominated over red pine in the proportion of about five to one. In the natural course of events the lumber trade has given place to agriculture, and the era of saw mills has almost departed. In a few of the northern townships, however, especially around Lake Couchiching, some mills of considerable proportions still flourish.

AGRICULTURE AND COMMERCE.

The greater part of the original forest in the district having been removed, fully half of the population live directly by agriculture. Along the lake shore the ground is stony and in many places still wooded ; where this wooded strip has been cleared it is chiefly used for pasture. At a short distance from the water, however, the land becomes arable and fit for farming purposes.

Ordinary lines of business are followed by the remainder of the population. The lake is almost surrounded by branches of the Grand Trunk Railway which perform the carrying trade, its steam craft being mostly used for merely local traffic, for towing timber, and for pleasure.

THE ICE INDUSTRY.

In winter Lake Simcoe is usually the scene of busy ice-harvesting operations. Its ice is always of first-class quality and from twelve to twenty inches thick. On two occasions—in the winter of

1879-80 and again in that of 1889-90—great
quantities of ice were sent from the lake to other
parts of Canada and to the United States, the mild-
ness of these winters causing the dealers to come
north for their supplies.   In the latter winter, viz.,
1889-90, cutting ice was conducted on a very extensive scale at Jackson's Point, Barrie and Orillia,
at which places the railway branches touch the
lake.   Five large ice companies from the States
had united on that occasion for the purpose of ob-
taining their season's supplies.   This Ice Union
was the largest concern of its kind in the world, its
members supplying New York, Rochester, Buffalo,
Cincinnati, and nearly all the leading cities of the
eastern states.   They had the most improved ma-
chinery for cutting and harvesting the ice.   Long
slides were made so that the blocks could be run
out of the water into the cars or the icehouses, some
of the slides being operated by endless chains
driven by steam.

So great was the quantity taken out that there
were not enough facilities for shipment over the
railways.   Thus large icehouses of boards had to
be erected along the shore for storing purposes,
until it could be removed as opportunity afforded,
several acres of ground being covered by these
structures.

Toronto firms now cut their supplies every
winter at Jackson's Point and Bell Ewart, at both
of which places branch railways touch the lake.

FISH AND GAME.

From the Dominion Government Blue Books
we learn each year the products of the Lake Simcoe
fisheries.   The figures of two late years may be
given as examples:—

KIND.	LBS., 1890.	LBS.. 1891.
Whitefish	1 500	——
Trout	32 500	28 000
Herring	10 000	10 000
Sturgeon	——	28 000
Maskinonge	26 300	——
Bass	43 400	45 000
Pickerel	7 000	7 000
Pike	43 000	53 000
Coarse Fish	25 000	28 000
Value	$11 492	$11 270

Maskinonge appear to be more abundant in
Lake Couchiching and the Severn River than elsewhere, and a few have been caught weighing as

high as 47 lbs. Speckled trout are abundant in the streams emptying into the lake. An improvement in the yield of whitefish within late years is ascribed to artificial restocking from the Government hatcheries. During late years considerable quantities of salmon trout fry have also been transferred to the lake from the Government fish breeding establishment at Newcastle, Ont. In 1890, these were distributed as follows :—Barrie, 200,000 ; Orillia, 200,000 ; Lefroy, 50,000. In addition to these, 100,000 whitefish fry were also placed at Lefroy in the same year.

In 1891, 100,000 salmon trout fry were placed in the lake at Barrie, 200,000 at Orillia, and 100,000 in Lake Conchiching. Of whitefish, the same year, 300,000 were placed at each of these towns,

Poachers sometimes violate the fishery laws, but are in almost every case brought to justice. The heavy fines imposed during recent years have had a telling effect, so that illegal fishing with nets or spears has almost ceased. Many nets have been confiscated and destroyed by the fishery overseers. Some mill-owners are reported to be still careless about the disposal of their sawdust and other rubbish which are detrimental to the fisheries. The overseers have of late years prosecuted several parties for allowing sawdust to escape into the rivers and streams, with a wholesome effect.

The Severn River is annually frequented by large numbers of anglers from the States, a single party in 1889 from Pittsburg, Pa., numbering over one hundred persons.

In *Prairie and Forest*, Parker Gilmore says :— "The best pike fishing I have ever enjoyed in my life was in the Holland River, about thirty miles north of Toronto, near its junction with Lake Simcoe. Here the fish are very large, and if caught in a taking humor the most greedy for sport will have their appetite abundantly satisfied. The eye of the connoisseur in piscatorial matters could not find a stream better suited in every particular for becoming the habitat of the pike than the river just mentioned, for it is densely margined with weeds on both sides, with a deep sluggish channel between them, and such are its characteristic features for many a mile. If the sportsman visited this haunt in spring or autumn, he should not fail to have his gun with him, tor innumerable wild fowl frequent it in their migrations North and South ; in fact, at sunset and break of day I have seen the entire surface of its placid waters covered with them.   Deer, also, were formerly very abundant here, but I fear that such is not now the case.   I can remember as if it were but yesterday, although twenty or more years have slipped past since then, I was on the upper deck of a steamboat, talking to its skipper, while the obedient vessel carefully threaded the erratic course of the Holland River, when my companion exclaimed, 'Here comes a buck !' and darted for the wheel-house ; in an instant he rejoined me, rifle in hand ; for some minutes we lost sight of the beauti- ful deer in the tall reeds, but soon afterward had the satisfaction of seeing him breasting the waves as he headed for the opposite bank.   The game be- ing behind us, pitching and tossing in the ground- swell caused by the passage of our craft, the captain delayed firing till the deer gained the margin ; in the halt that he made to recover his strength, the better to be able to withdraw his feet from the sticky, muddy bottom, the rifle was slowly brought to bear upon the quarry's heart, and with the report the gallant animal gave a tremendous struggle, and pitched headlong, to rise no more."

Of the larger kinds of game, black bears are still common, as also red deer; but most of the latter, as well as their enemies the wolves, have retreated farther north with the disappearance of the forests from the district.   Some of the smaller fur-bearing animals are still abundant in some places, such as minks, muskrats, etc.   Partridges are numerous in the woods of the district, and ducks frequent the marshes in considerable numbers, as well as other kinds of small waterfowl, duck-shooting being a favorite sport in the autumn.

THE INDIANS.

The remnant of the red men, who once fre- quented the lake in such large numbers, now oc- cupy two reserves :   (1) The Lake Simcoe Agency comprising Snake and Georgina Islands, and (2) The Rama Reserve.

The Indians on both of these reserves are Chippewas.

Those of Georgina and Snake Islands have made a commendable advance toward material wealth and now are an intelligent and moral community. Until recently the Indian Agent, there, was Mr. J. R. Stevenson of Georgina, whose annual reports to the Department of Indian Affairs are full of useful intelligence on the state of the band under his charge. The population of this agency is about one hundred and twenty-five, and their premises are kept in a neat and tidy condition. There are now only two families living on Snake Island, but it used to be thickly peopled, all the others having removed to Georgina Island. Snake Island has an area of 400 acres, is prettily situated, being distant three-quarters of a mile from the mainland of the County of York. It remains chiefly in pasture land, but a large portion of it is covered with a beautiful forest of second growth timber. Georgina Island is cultivated and contains the dwellings of most of the band. The Chief is Chas. Big Canoe who has held the office for four terms. According to the agent, "generally speaking the band is very prosperous, earning a comfortable living, adding materially to their stock of worldly goods, and surrounding themselves with many comforts unknown to them in former days." Agriculture is the leading industry. Abundant crops are harvested every year, attention is paid to gardening, and live stock in good condition is constantly kept. In addition to this, an extensive industry has arisen from the manufacture of baskets, which are sold or traded in the towns and villages surrounding the lake. Another industry, the gathering of ginseng, has lately proved profitable to the band, $1,000 worth alone having been shipped from Georgina in 1890. The school here is conducted under the auspices of the Methodist Missionary Society. The band is credited with $24,600 in the Indian Trust Fund of the Dominion.

The population of the Rama agency is about 235. The Indian Agent is Mr. D. J. McPhee of Uptergrove, who reports that "consumption is the prevalent disease to which they are subject, and it is slowly but surely decreasing their numbers." In agriculture they are making fair progress. "During the summer months a number of these Indians are constantly employed as guides to tourists and pleasure-seekers, by whom they are well paid, some of them earning as much as $60 per month." Like the Georgina Indians, this band also gathered and sold in 1890 as much as $5,000 worth of ginseng root. The band might be described as on a good footing were it not for the facility with which some of its members can obtain intoxicants. Efforts, however, are made for the suppression of this violation by white men of the liquor clauses of the Indian Act. The Chief of the band is J. B. Naningishkung. As at Georgina, the school at Rama is also under the auspices of the Methodist Missionary Society. The band is credited with $53,000 in the Indian Trust Fund.

CHAPTER III.

A CIRCUIT AROUND THE LAKE.

HOLLAND LANDING.

BEGINNING at the southwestern corner of the lake, the Holland River, with its historical associations, will deserve more than a passing notice. Leaving Cook's Bay, and following up stream the east branch of the river, the first landmark of importance that one finds is the old Soldiers' Landing, also known as the Lower or Steamboat landing. This was used during the war of 1812–15 ; and for many years after the expiration of the war a number of cannons were left here in charge of a soldier. They were afterwards removed by the Government. They had been brought here as the " Landing " was the point at which all heavy goods in transit over the Great Portage from Lake Ontario to Lake Huron were placed on board the large batteaux for transporta-

tion across Lake Simcoe. Here, too, the well-
known anchor of such enormous dimensions remained for many years as a memento of the war
time. But, like the cannons, it has also been
removed, though not to a great distance. A few
years ago it was hauled with much difficulty from
the Lower Landing to the village park near the

THE ANCHOR AT HOLLAND LANDING.

Upper Landing, where it now rests. This gigantic
anchor came from His Majesty's dockyards in
England, and was intended for a large frigate that
was under construction at Drummond Island, in
Lake Huron. On its way thither it had reached
the Holland Landing by the assistance of sixteen
yoke of oxen, when peace came and interrupted
all further operations at the "Navy Yard" on
Drummond Island. Being too large for transporta-
tion (its length is $15\frac{1}{2}$ feet, excluding the ring),
except under the most urgent circumstances, the

anchor brought thus far on its way was left at Holland Landing, where it now remains to form a curious monument of those early stirring times.

Afterward, when regular navigation opened on Lake Simcoe, the Lower Landing was used for the larger vessels and steamers. At this place the Holland River was about twenty-five yards wide, its banks being low and marshy, and thickly wooded with tamarac. It was at this uninviting place that Yonge Street, the great colonization highway, terminated. and merged into the water course across Lake Simcoe. Dr. Scadding, one of our most entertaining Canadian historians, thus pictures, in his *Tororto of Old*, the Lower Landing as it appeared before it fell into its present deserted condition :

" In a clear space on the right, there were some long low buildings of log, with strong shutters on the windows, usually closed. These were the Government depositories of naval and military stores, and Indian presents, on their way to Penetanguishene. The cluster of buildings here was once known as Fort Gwillimbury. Thus we have it written in the old *Gazetteer* of 1799 : 'It is thirty miles from York to Holland River, at the Pine Fort called Gwillimbury, where the road ends.' "

Many early travellers of distinction visited the Lower Landing in the course of their journeys, and have left records of the scenes they beheld. Amongst these have been La Salle, Sir Geo. Head, Sir John Franklin, John Galt, Capt. Basil Hall, and a score of less noted persons.

The open space referred to, in the above extract, was used as a camping-ground by the early Indians and fur-traders. Here could be seen encamped at all seasons of the year large numbers of Indians, often from very remote districts on the upper lakes. Many of these came several times a year for the purpose of bartering their furs at Holland Landing, which was a sort of emporium for a large part of the northern country. Here, too, the annual distributions of presents to the Indians were made at first. The ceremony was witnessed by the distinguished traveller Capt. Basil Hall on July 20th, 1827, and he has described it in an interesting manner in his *Travels in North America in* 1827-1828. The distribution for the year 1828 took place on

August 14th, and a description of it has been left
us by the native preacher, Rev. Peter Jones. (*Life
and Journals.* Page 164.)

Continuing our journey up stream, the next
landmark reached is the Upper or Canoe Landing,
which is about a mile and a half above the Steamboat Landing. This Upper Landing was the
ancient Indian place of embarkation of the war-
parties and hunting-parties ; and after the white
men came upon these scenes it was still used as the
landing place for canoes and lighter craft which
could get higher up the stream than the Steamboat
Landing. A small bytown, consisting of two or
three business places, arose at the Upper Landing
at an early date—sometime in the twenties.

About a mile and a half above the Upper or
Canoe Landing arose the village of Holland
Landing itself—the early commercial distributing
point for Simcoe. Until 1853, however, it was
known as St. Albans, and sometimes as Beverly.
The opening of the Northern Railway took
place in June of that year. According to the last
census (1891), Holland Landing, which is an incorporated village, had a population of 443.

BRADFORD, on the West Branch of the
Holland, where the "Northern" Branch of the
Grand Trunk crosses the river, has a steamboat
landing. The village, which is incorporated, had a
population, when the last census was taken (1891)
of 996. It has, proportional to its size, the ordinary
branches of industry and lines of business. A daily
stage runs to Bond Head, 6 miles west. The
Holland River Marsh at this place has long been
celebrated for its abundance of wild fowl.

DE GRASSI POINT guards the entrance from
the lake to Cook's Bay, connection with Roach's
Point on the opposite shore being kept up by a
ferry. It affords a pleasant camping-ground in
summer, and is used for that purpose, a syndicate
of Toronto capitalists having purchased the ground
at the Point and laid it out for summer cottages of
which there are a number. The place is reached
from Lefroy station on the Railway. It was at this
Point that Canise, the Indian Chief and friend of
Governor Simcoe, died in 1793 [See Diary of Sheriff
Macdonell]. From time immemorial De Grassi
Point has been a favorite haunt of the Indians.

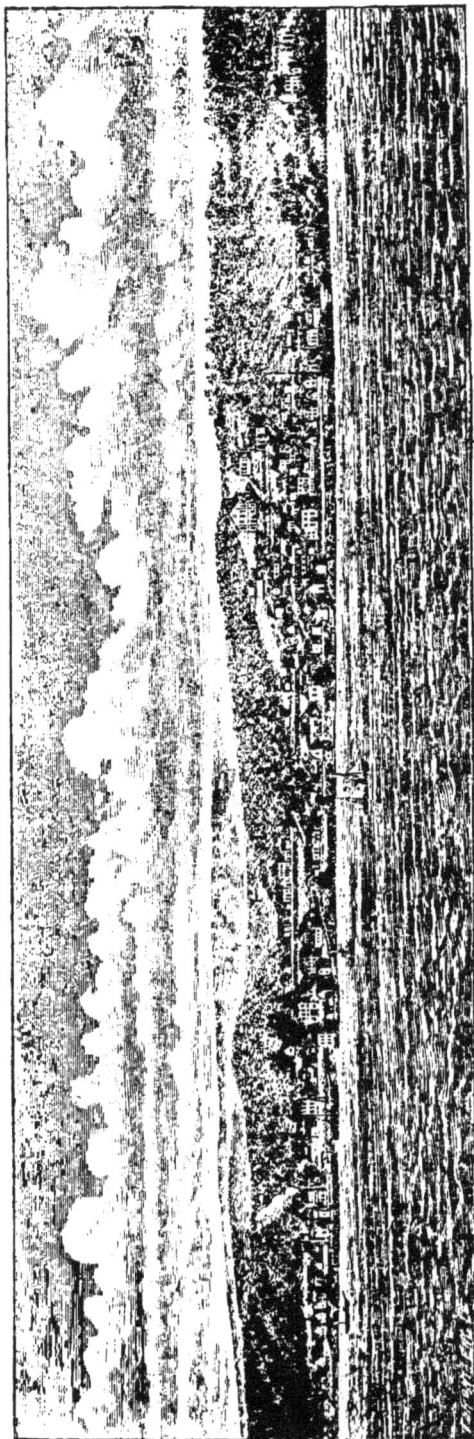

AN EARLY VIEW OF THE TOWN OF BARRIE (1853).

FROM A DRAWING BY THE LATE CAPT. W. H. GRUBBE.

BELL EWART, once the commercial metropolis of the Lake Simcoe region, is also reached from Lefroy station. For a long time, immediately succeeding the opening of the Northern Railway in 1853, it was the busiest distributing point in the North, two American capitalists having built a large saw mill there. While good timber was plentiful around the lake, a large business was carried on ; but after a few years the timber limits became partially exhausted, the large mill was accidentally burned down, and Bell Ewart dwindled away. In earlier years a spur line ran from the railway at Lefroy, and Bell Ewart was a regular station, but the branch railway was subsequently taken up. Another line of rails was, however, laid down in '92 for the purpose of shipping the large quantities of ice taken out at this place by Toronto merchants.

LAKELAND. With Bell Ewart the list of decayed villages is not exhausted, for about three miles to the north of that place, beyond Cedar Point, on the shore of a small bay, are to be seen the remains of what was once the small village of Lakeland. Here are the ruins of a sawmill and two or three dozen houses, but the place is now without a single human habitation.

SANDY COVE, about midway between Cedar Point and Big Bay Point, has a few summer residences. It was formerly a favorite camping ground of Indians.

KEMPENFELDT BAY.

BIG BAY POINT, owing to its lonely situation between the lake itself and Kempenfeldt Bay is a favorite summer resort. There are two large summer hotels at this place, both the work of private enterprise. One is situated in the centre of Peninsular Park (40 acres) and was established in 1887 at an expense of about $50,000. The other, the Robinson House, was built a few years ago by the late Isaac Robinson. The Point is finely wooded with a large second growth of maple, beech, pine, and butternut. Steamers ply daily during the summer months between this resort and Barrie, nine miles distant.

STRATHALLAN, about midway along the south shore of Kempenfeldt Bay, is the picturesque summer residence of the Hon. G. W. Allan, ex-Speaker of the Canadian Senate.

TOLLENDAL, farther west along the same shore, has many historical associations. Here was the spot where took place some of the scenes of the novel, "An Algonquin Maiden," written by Mr. G. Mercer Adam and Miss Wetherald. Situated at the outlet of a large stream, Tollendal has mills, besides a few private residences admirably located near the water.

ALLANDALE, incorporated as a village in 1891, is a busy Grand Trunk Railway centre Here are located the divisional headquarters and machine shops. Five branches radiate at this point : (1) the Northern from Toronto ; (2) the Northwestern from Hamilton ; (3) the Muskoka, which is the through line to the Pacific ; (4) the Penetanguishene branch, and (5) the Meaford branch. In the station lawn at Allandale, there is a bronze bust of the late Col. F. W. Cumberland, General Manager of the Northern Railway for twenty-two years. A wharf was constructed here in 1893,

BARRIE, pleasantly situated at the north-western corner of Kempenfeldt Bay, around the head of which the railway runs, presents a picturesque appearance when seen across the water. Its rows of brick houses and stores, its church spires and public buildings, all rising from the slope of an amphitheatre of hills, with boats in the bay and others lying by the wharves, make a delightful scene. During the summer season there is daily steamboat communication with Big Bay Point and other places on Lake Simcoe. Its population is 5,550. It had its beginning in 1832, became an incorporated village in 1853, and a town in 1871, having been the county seat since 1842.

SHANTY BAY. In passing down the north shore of the bay one sees a number of private residences picturesquely situated in park-like grounds near the water side. "Woodlands," the summer seat of Mr. Crawford, of St. Louis, Mo , was erected at a great expense by Mr. R. Power. Farther down is " The Woods," the residence of Col. W. E. O'Brien, M.P. At Shanty Bay, where its beautiful church is seen against a background of woods, there is a small wharf.

ORO STATION also has a small wharf, and the steamboats make occasional calls.

HAWKESTONE.   From an early date, Hodges'
Landing, now known as Hawkestone, has had an
important position amongst the landing places on
the north shore of the lake.   But it has always
suffered for want of a natural harbor.

SHINGLE BAY.   So early as 1834, a few
of the settlers made an attempt to establish a town
at Shingle Bay, and gave it the name of " Innisfallen," but the results of the scheme were far,
far short of their expectations.   Innisfallen never
came to anything more than a few cabins on the
shore, though the site chosen had much to com-
mend it in view of its picturesqueness.

GRAPE ISLAND—LAKE SIMCOE.

GRAPE ISLAND lies off the entrance to " The
Narrows" at the head of Lake Simcoe.   Landing
places at the northernmost end of the lake were various
in early times, but all were continuative of the great
highway across the province at this part.   In the
immediate vicinity of " The Narrows " there were
three, at least, of these early landing places : One

at Shingle Bay, just mentioned ; The Narrows
proper, where the scattered hamlet of Invermara
marks the place where a crossing was effected ;
while the third was on the shore of Lake Couchiching, where Orillia now stands.   Facing the lake
at this part are the large buildings of the Ontario
Asylum for Idiots.

LAKE COUCHICHING.

" The Narrows," the water channel between
Lake Simcoe and Lake Couchiching, is crossed by
swing bridges on the railway and the public highway.   Couchiching Park (180 acres), on the west
side, was laid out through the enterprise of the
late Col. Cumberland, General Manager of the
" Northern," and may be called the first attempt of
any magnitude to open up this north land for summer tourists.   The large hotel in this park was
burned down about 1877, but private residences now
occupy the beautiful peninsula.   It was here that
the late Hon. John Hillyard Cameron, the eminent
Toronto counsel, while attending a court at Orillia
in October, 1876, imprudently bathed in the cold
waters of the Narrows and contracted an illness
which proved fatal.

ORILLIA is beautifully situated upon a hill-
side at the southwestern part of Lake Couchiching.
The town, which has a population of 4,752 according
to the census of 1891, was incorporated in 1874 and
has always been popular as a summer resort.
The American Canoe Club met at Horse Shoe
Island in the summer of 1892.   Steamers ply daily
to points on Lake Couchiching and to Strawberry
Island, eight miles distant.   At various times the
town of Orillia has figured in Canadian literature.
Mrs. Anna Jameson, the distinguished authoress,
passed that way in 1837, and recorded her ex-
periences in *Winter Studies and Summer Rambles*
(Vol. 3).   Charles Sangster's familiar " Sonnets
written in the Orillia woods, August, 1859," were
composed during a prolonged visit with friends
near the place.   Dr. Scadding, the distinguished
historian of Toronto, has also, on various occasions,
written upon Orillia and its surroundings.

GENEVA PARK, on a point stretching out into
Lake Couchiching, seven miles from Orillia, is a

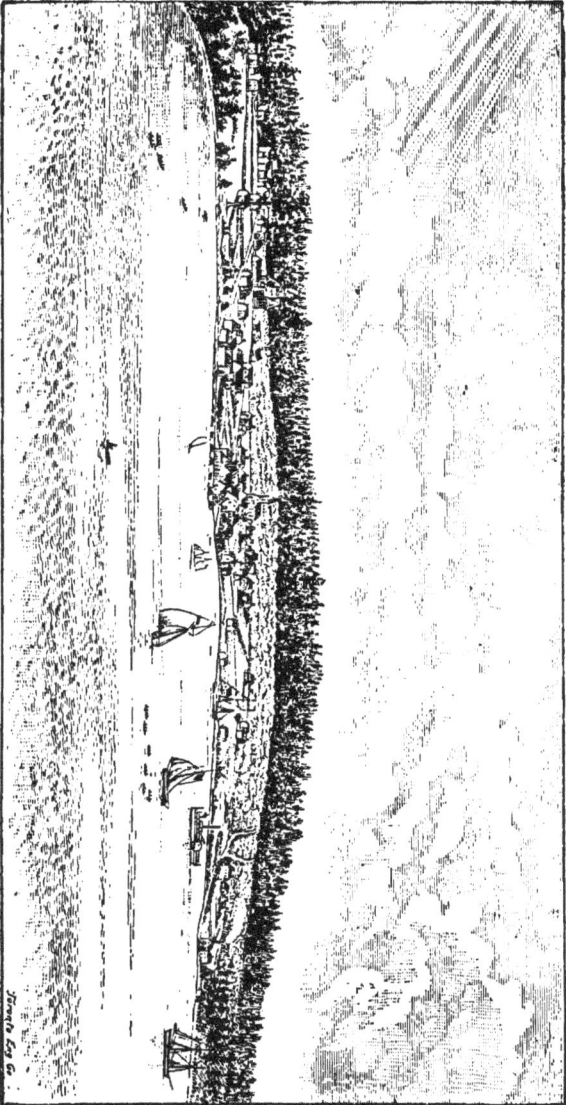

AN EARLY VIEW OF THE TOWN OF ORILLIA (1854)

FROM A DRAWING BY THE LATE CAPT. W. H. GRUBBE.

pretty lake resort. It is well wooded with maple, and has conveniences for camping.

LONGFORD is noted for its extensive lumbering operations. Lake St. John in the neighborhood is a small sheet of water connected with Lake Couchiching by a Portage for logs. The famous quarries here were established many years ago, chiefly through the enterprise of the late Lieut. Allan Macpherson. He died in 1859, and the business has since been carried on by his descendants.

RAMA. A place of interest is the settlement of Ojibbeway Indians on their reserve at Rama. It dates from 1838, when Chief Yellowhead and his band removed from the Narrows and purchased 1600 acres of land in Rama for £800. A Wesleyan mission to these Indians was established at an early period, and here have labored at successive times : Wm. Herkimer, Thomas Hurlburt, George Mc-Dougall and other noted missionaries.

ATHERLEY, on the east side of "The Narrows," is on the Midland division of the Grand Trunk Railway. As long ago as the beginning of this century, Mr. Quetton St. George had a trading-post near Atherley for the Indians. In the Public Library, Toronto, there is preserved a manuscript note book which did service at this early trading-post. It bears the date, 1802.

STRAWBERRY ISLAND has been converted into a pleasant summer resort by Capt. C. McInnes of Orillia. It was formerly called Starvation Island from the fact that about a dozen Indians were starved to death there sometime in the last century, their canoes having been washed away during a storm.

THORAH ISLAND, containing 1450 acres, was formerly an Indian Reserve, but is now occupied by white people. It was once named "Canise Island ;" this name, however, has failed to come into general use. The Thorah Island camping party of Toronto make annual visits to the place.

BEAVERTON, at the southeastern part of Lake Simcoe, has a population of 850, and was incorporated as a village in 1884. An extensive wharf was built here in 1891 at a cost of about $9,000, and a breakwater in the following year. The original settlers here were chiefly Highland Scotch.

DUCLOS' POINT, to the southeast of Georgina Is'and. is a long point running out into the lake.

GEORGINA ISLAND bears the name of a daughter of Governor Simcoe. It was originally called Graves Island, but this name did not come into

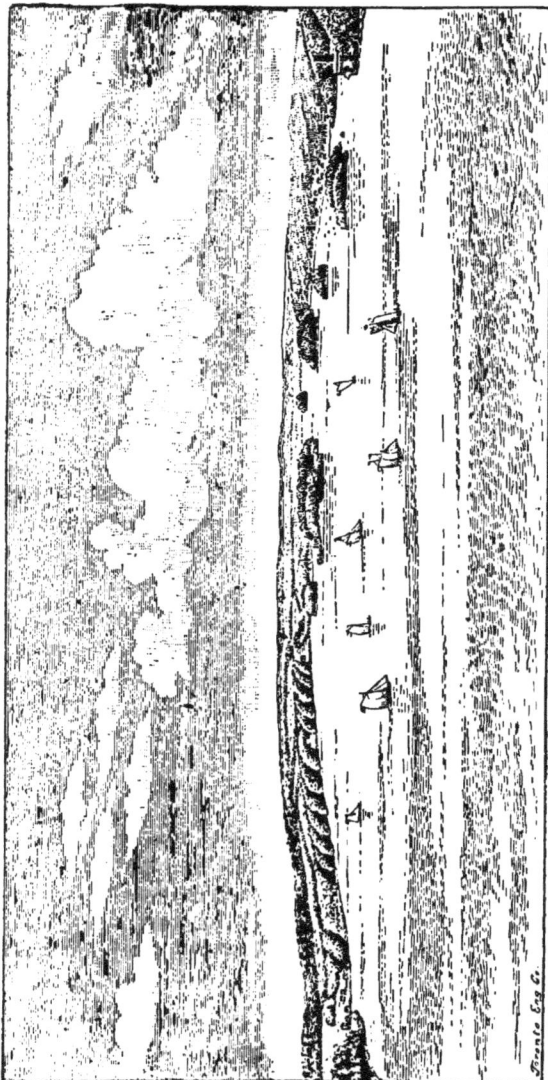

A VIEW OF LAKE COUCHICHING

common use. It has an area of about 2,000 acres, and is wholly an Indian Reserve. The channel between the island and the mainland is now much deeper than it was some years ago, which is a striking instance of the effects of lake-currents.

JACKSON'S POINT is named from a noted early resident of that place, of whom Dr. Scadding in his *Toronto of Old* gives a sketch of considerable length. A public park was opened here in June, 1888. At Sibbald Point, near by, is a pretty stone church, erected as a memorial to the wife of the late Capt. Sibbald, R.N.

SUTTON village (incorporated), with a population of 686, is a short distance from the shore. It was originally called "Bourchier's Mills." On the lake shore are many summer cottages, and for an outing the place is a favorite one with citizens of Toronto, to which it is convenient by railway. Quantities of ice are taken in winter from the lake at this point, especially for shipment to Toronto.

SNAKE ISLAND is an Indian Reserve, as also is Fox Island. There is a lighthouse on the latter.

ROACH'S POINT, nine miles west of Jackson's Point, is at the entrance to Cook's Bay. Many historical associations cling to this place, which has been a conspicuous landmark since the district was first settled.

KESWICK, a short distance to the south, is a resort of long standing. Near here is the noted residence named "Beechcroft," erected about 1872 at an enormous expense by Mr. A. G. P. Dodge. Several wealthy Toronto families have summer residences on the lake shore at this place.

Miscellaneous Sketches of the Lake.

GOVERNOR SIMCOE'S VISIT IN 1793.

[The 1891 volume of the Transactions of the Canadian Institute contains a Diary of Governor Simcoe's Journey from Humber Bay to Penetanguishene in 1793. The Diary is that of Sheriff Macdonell, who accompanied Governor Simcoe on that occasion, the manuscript of which is in the possession of Alex. Macdonell, Clerk of Process at Osgoode Hall, and a son of the writer. A few extracts from the diary were read before the Historical section of the Canadian Institute, on Jan. 15th, '91. by William Houston, M.A., ex-Librarian of the Legislative Library, through whose instrumentality it has since been published. Mr. Macdonell's account of their passage through Lake Simcoe is here given.]

" At twenty minutes after one, (Sept. 29th, 1793), we entered Lake LaClaie, now Lake Simcoe, so called in memory of Captain Simcoe of the R.N. At the entrance of the lake we saw two canoes, who upon seeing us, paddled off to their village, which was upon a point about four miles off, [evidently what is now known as DeGrassi Point, which has always been a rendezvous for Indians], to apprise them of the Governor's arrival. We paddled on towards the point and passed the village close in shore. The Indians who were by this time assembled, fired a *feu de joie* to compliment his Excellency, which we answered with three cheers, and then doubled the point, and put on shore in a small sandy bay to dine. Soon after our landing the Indians came in a body to wait on the Governor, to whom they presented a beaver blanket, which he declined taking then, but promised to take it upon his return from Matchetache Bay. They were all more or less drunk and made rather an unintelligible speech. They got liquor from four Canadians who had been sent from Matchetache Bay by Cowan, an Indian trader, to buy corn. His Excellency was sorry that he could not see Keenees the chief of the village, with whom he was acquainted, as he was dangerously ill. We left our small canoe here, and got one Indian in lieu of the two Indians belonging to the village, who preferred remaining to proceeding on the journey. After dinner we re-embarked, and the wind being fair, hoisted sail, and about dark put on shore and encamped in a cedar grove about six miles from the village. [This would be at or near what is now known as Cedar Point.]

30th—Left our encampment about ten o'clock. Mr. Givens was taken into the Governor's canoe, and in his place one of the rangers put into mine. Sailed on with a strong breeze about six miles, and it blowing too fresh to cross Kempenfeldt Bay, put in at Point Endeavour, [Big Bay Point], where we remained till two o'clock, and dined. After dinner, the wind moderating a little, we again hoisted sail and crossed the bay, which is between seven and eight miles deep and four and five wide. We had scarcely got over when the wind blew hard ahead, and it beginning to rain we encamped in a pleasant spot on the side of the lake. [This would be near Hawkstone of the present].

October 1st—Embarked about eight o'clock, and having a contrary wind had to paddle against a head swell, which impeded our going much, and frequently dashed water into our canoes. Put in for a few minutes to take the bearings at a bluff point about six miles from our last encampment. This being accomplished we coasted close in shore for some time and, the wind abating, made for an island near the head of the lake, and landed there about two o'clock, and dined. This island, now Francis's Island, is pleasantly situated, having a fine prospect of the lake. The Indians used to raise corn upon it but have not for some time. It is quite covered with long grass. About two o'clock we embarked and shortly after leaving the island entered a small straight [The Narrows], near the

far extremity of which we saw two Indians in a
canoe paddling across. Soon as the Indian in the
Governor's canoe perceived them he gave a death
hallow ; the strange Indians made for land, and we,
seeing the wigwam, followed. Soon as our Indian
got near enough to be heard he made a melancholy
detail of the number of deaths that had lately
happened among the Lake Simcoe Indians, and
closed his speech by saying "that the end of the
world was at hand, Indians would be no more."
An old Indian, owner of the wigwam, gave a similar
unpleasant account of the great sickness in his
neighborhood also, and added that he expected his
eldest son would soon change his climate, and that
nothing but his being unwell prevented his going
to his wintering ground. His excellency made this
family a small present, and we parted. Soon after
leaving them, the wind turning fair, we hoisted sail.
At this place the lake widens, and is interspersed
with small islands, on some of which the Indians
had planted corn, turnips and squashes. About
sunset got to the head of the lake, entered the River
Matchetache [Severn], and encamped.

[Four days were occupied in going from this
place to "Matchetache Bay" by way of the Severn,
an account of the journey being preserved in the
Diary. On the return trip, the party reached the
same spot at the head of Lake Couchiching on Oct.
8th, and encamped. The entry for the following
day then reads :]

9th—Embarked after breakfast, and having
paddled against a head wind and swell arrived at
Francis' Island at twelve o'clock. His Excellency
did intend going from this island round the opposite
side of the lake to what we had come, but finding
only four days' provisions remaining, and not know-
ing what time it would take us by so doing, he
judged it more expedient to return by the way we
had come ; therefore, after dinner got on board,
crossed to the main land and before sunset encamped where we had slept on the 30th September.

10th—Got into our canoes before sunrise, being
fearful that we would have the wind ahead and
wishing to cross Kempenfeldt Bay before it blew too
hard. Our apprehensions were confirmed. The
wind began to rise, but we luckily got over the bay
before the lake was too rough. Put on shore and

breakfasted at Endeavour Point. Re-embarked and coasted along shore. At one o'clock put in, and dined about two miles' distance from the village. Having dined and got on board we paddled on and soon came abreast of the village. The Indians fired a *feu de joie*, and we gave three cheers. Got round the point, put on shore in a small bay, hauled our canoes on shore and encamped in the rear of the village. While we were making up the fires and preparing everything for the night His Excellency humanely went to pay a visit to Keenees, the chief, who, as I have already mentioned, was dangerously ill when we had passed on our way to Matchetache Bay, but on getting to his wigwam he was informed that he had been dead some days. A man possessed of less sensibility and feelings than the Governor would have been shocked on this occasion, but his were plainly painted on his countenance upon his return to camp. About six o'clock a number of squaws came to visit the Governor. Two of them carried the images of their deceased husbands, dolls about two feet long decorated with silver broaches, feathers, paint, &c, if a chief, as was the case with one of these (Keenees), his medal is hung to his neck, the face painted black. His Excellency gave them some knives and looking-glasses, and shortly after they retired. At 8 o'clock the Indians came in a body, and being seated around the fire got a dram and a piece of tobacco, after which the chief got up, thanked the Great Father, and presented him with the beaver blanket, which he spread under him. He then said : "You white men pray ; we poor Indians do not know what it is, but we hope you will entreat the Great Spirit to remove the sickness from amongst us." To which the Governor replied that they should certainly be remembered in the prayers of the whites. He then ordered them a keg of rum, and they went away perfectly happy, and highly pleased that the blanket was accepted, and that they had made their Father's bed.

11th—About 9 o'clock left our encampment, embarked, and soon got out of the lake."

CAPTAIN BASIL HALL AT HOLLAND LAND-
ING IN 1827.

[Captain Basil Hall, R.N., in his passage through Canada in 1827, made a digression from his western course to Holland Landing to witness the annual distribution of presents to the Indians which took place there on July 20th of that year. Hall's account of this distribution is interesting inasmuch as it describes the ornaments in use at that time by the Chippe-was of Lake Simcoe. The account is given below in full, and is taken from his "Travels in North America in the years 1827 and 1828, vol. I, p. 253."]

On the 19th day of July, instead of proceeding, as we had intended, straight along the great road to the eastward, we made a sharp turn to the left, and travelled for some thirty miles directly north towards Lake Simcoe, one of those numerous sheets of water with which Upper Canada is covered ; and destined, no doubt in after times, to afford the means of much valuable intercourse from place to place, when their banks are peopled and cultivated. Our present object, however, was to witness the annual distribution of presents, as they are called, made by government to the Indians ; the regular payment, in short, of the annuities, in consideration of which, the Indians have agreed to relinquish their title to lands in certain parts of the country.

*   *   *   *   *   *

The scene at Holland Landing was amusing enough, for there were collected about three hundred Indians, with their squaws and papooses, as the women and children are called. Some of the party were encamped under the brush wood, in birch-bark wigwams, or huts, but the greater number, having paddled down Lake Simcoe in the morning, had merely drawn up their canoes on the grass, ready to start again as soon as the ceremonies of the day were over. The Indian agent seemed to have hard work to arrange the party to his mind ; but at length the men and woman were placed in separate lines, while the children lay sprawling and bawling in the middle. Many of the males, as well as females, wore enormous earrings, some of which I found, upon admeasurement, to be six inches in length ; and others carried round their necks silver ornaments, from the size of a watch, to that of a soup-plate. Sundry damsels, I suppose at the top of the fashion, had strung over them more than a dozen of necklaces of variously stained glass beads.

One man, I observed was ornamented with a set of
bones, described to me as the celebrated wampum,
of which everyone has heard ; and this personage
with four or five others, and a few of the women,
were wired in the nose like pigs, with rings which
dangled against their lips. Such of the papooses
as were not old enough to run about and take care
of themselves, were strapped up in boxes, with nothing exposed but their heads and toes. So that
when the mothers were too busy to attend to their
offspring the little animals might be hooked up
out of the way, upon the nearest branch of a tree,
or placed against a wall, like a hat or a pair of
boots, and left there to squall away to their hearts
content.

JOHN GALT ON LAKE SIMCOE IN 1827.

INTERESTING SKETCH BY THE FAMOUS TRAVEL-
LER. REPRINTED FROM HIS AUTO-
BIOGRAPHY, VOL, 2. P. 72.

[The following sketch of a tour through this lake in 1827 by the
famous John Galt will be sufficiently new to most of our readers to warrant
its republication at this remote date. He was on a tour of inspection to
Goderich at the time, by way of Penetanguishene, to the lands of the
Canada Company in Bruce and Huron counties.]

Next morning we went forward to a place on
the Holland River called Holland's Landing, an
open space which the Indians and fur-traders
were in the habit of frequenting. It presented to
me something of a Scottish aspect in the style of
the cottages ; but instead of mountains the environs
were covered with trees. We embarked at this
place. After descending the river we steered across
Lake Simcoe, the boatmen during the time amused
us in the stillness of the evening with those French
airs which Moore has rendered so popular by his
Canadian boat songs. At a dark, if not a late hour,
we reached a house frequented by the Indian
traders, where we stayed the remainder of the
night. Our reception was very primitive, but the
civility of the inmates did much to reconcile us to
the best they could give. In point of accommoda-
tion it reminded me of a night spent long ago in
Greece, on the shores of the gulph of Euboea, but

the comparison, though not much, was in favor of
the Grecian cottage. By dawn of day we were informed that the boatmen were ready, and immediately embarked. A vapour lay on the tops of
the trees, and circumscribed our view, showing
enough, however, to remind us that we were in a
far country. The mist prevented me from seeing
the outlines of the adjacent lands, but the situation
of the house reminded me of Rhuardinnan at the
foot of Ben Lomond in Scotland. Our progress
over the still lake in a fresh and serene morning was
delightful ; not a breath ruffled the face of the
waters, and all around us " Looked tranquility." In
this little voyage I remember an incident which at
the time impressed me with curious emotion. A
vast moth as big as a bird flew over the boat in
perfect silence, its course and appearance was not
like any "creature of the element," and my imagination exalted it into an imp of darkness
flying homeward.

We then turned to the coast of Innesfail, on
which I had a grant of land, but as we had a long
voyage and journey before us, we only touched
there to speak to a settler who hailed us as we
passed. From him I learned that several clearances,
as the cutting down of the timber is called, were
then afoot, and a few settlers had recently arrived.
Having conversed with him some time we steered
for Kempenfeldt Bay, and had another sight that
could only be met with in America, a squaw with
several Indian children, crossing the lake in a canoe
steered by a negro! My imagination surely was
given to dark fancies, for I could not help compar-
ing the transit of this party in that grey and silent
morning, with something or another, I will not say,
a " better world." We ascended Kempenfeldt Bay,
or more properly Gulph, nearly to the head, where
we met horses with our luggage, which had come
through the forest by a tract recently opened, a
great convenience in summer ; in winter the lake is
frozen, and travellers pass on the ice. From the
spot where we disembarked, I proceeded along a
road which was opened by a party during the late
war under the command of Dr. Dunlop, whom I
was to meet on Lake Huron, but the forest glade
was nearly again impassable by the new vegetation,
and we were obliged to travel it in single file.

A REMINISCENCE OF KEMPENFELDT BAY.

GLOWING DESCRIPTION OF ITS PICTURESQUE SHORES, AND SHANTY BAY, AS THEY APPEARED FIFTY YEARS AGO.

[The autumn of 1842 will be remembered by Canadians of three-score years, as a time of extraordinary beauty. The glowing tints of the forests, the calm and silent waters, and the many features peculiar to Indian summer, were more beautiful than usual. Its lovliness has been chronicled by the well-known American writer, Nathaniel Hawthorne, whose pen has preserved so many other features characteristic of this continent. It was in October of that year that Rev. S. B. Ardagh first arrived at Shanty Bay, which was to be his home for so many years. A most interesting reminis-cence from the pen of his daughter appeared in the Memoir of that lamented gentleman a few years ago. It is herewith reproduced by permission, and will doubtless be highly appreciated by our readers.]

"How vividly upon my memory are photo-graphed the recollections of those days of travel. The sluggish Holland River, whose pale marsh grasses undulated with the movement of the paddle-wheels ; the broad bright lake, the noble estuary of Kempenfeldt Bay, whose far-stretching shores, broken in outline by bay and headland, were vestured and crowned with the glory of the autumn woods. Four miles from the entrance, on the north shore, we steamed up to the wharf at Shanty Bay, a rude wooden pier, the foreground of a sylvan recess surrounded by wooded heights. The face of these low cliffs was clothed with the luxuriant foliage of wild raspberry and vine, and through their tangled bloom rocky paths led to the road above, a road by courtesy only, it being a chaos of mud holes, dry in hot weather, and bridged over by 'corduroys' in hopelessly miry places. Here we always found the earliest wild violets and hepaticas of spring, and its picturesque woodland scenery atoned for the marshy condition of the pathway. Two days later, in company with our kind host and hostess, and their children, we attended our first service in the church at Shanty Bay, embarked at the same rustic wharf, in order to avoid the worst half of the road to the church, then almost impass-able from recent rains. The affluance of light and color which characterized that Indian summer, made a vivid impression on those fresh from a paler and less glowing atmosphere. Here we saw, in all their beauty, the brilliant clearness of the inland waters, the circling ring of green woods surrounding the

'clearing' where we landed, where, from the sombre
hues of the ancient pine forests, and the brighter
tints of later growth, gleamed out the crimson and
gold, the russet and purple of a Canadian autumn.
In the background of the clearing the little white
church seemed to nestle in the bosom of the woods;
whilst in the foreground the tiny rustic parsonage,
surrounded by *debris*, fallen timber, and stumps of
trees, indicative of a new clearing, and itself half
veiled by low shrubbery, trailing Virginia creeper,
and tall rank grasses, was not out of unison with the
wildness of the surrounding landscape.   Many will
remember this sunny spot at a later time, when, in
a still rustic, but more ample habitation, with long,
low, vine-covered verandah, a host of friends were
generally found and always welcome.   The surroundings had then more the aspect of lawn and
garden ; and at the foot of the green-sloping land
the water chimed and murmured through the
summer days, or broke in a louder resonance on
autumn nights.   The little point of silvery pebbles
which stretched into the blue water to the right of
the Parsonage, was called by the little ones 'Rosy'
Point, because of the bloom of wild roses, which
blended with the emerald foliage of early summer.
Towards this, and along the shore, ran a shady,
woodland walk, so close to the lake that in spring,
when the waters were high, the waves often broke
over the pathway."

SANGSTER'S "WOODS NEAR ORILLIA."

My footsteps press where, centuries ago,
  The Red Men fought and conquered; lost and won,
Whole tribes and races, gone like last year's snow,
  Have found the Eternal Hunting-Grounds, and run
The fiery gauntlet of their active days,
  Till few are left to tell the mournful tale;
And these inspire us with such wild amaze
  They seem like spectres passing down a vale
Steep'd in uncertain moonlight, on their way
Towards some bourn where darkness blinds the day,
And night is wrapped in mystery profound.
  We cannot lift the mantle of the past;
We seem to wander over hallow'd ground;
  We scan the trail of Thought but all is overcast.

There was A TIME—and that is all we know.
  No record lives of their ensanguin'd deeds;
The past seems palsied with some giant blow,
  And grows the more obscure on what it feeds,
A rotted fragment of a human leaf;
  A few stray skulls; a heap of human bones!
These are the records—the traditions brief—
  "Twere easier far to read the speechless stones.
The fierce Ojibways, with tornado force,
  Striking white terror to the hearts of braves !
The mighty Hurons, rolling on their course,
  Compact and steady as the ocean waves;
The fiery Iroquois, a warrior host;
  Who were they ? whence ? and why ? no human tongue can boast !